FACE PAINTING

Devised and illustrated by

Clare Beaton

WARWICK PRESS

Contents

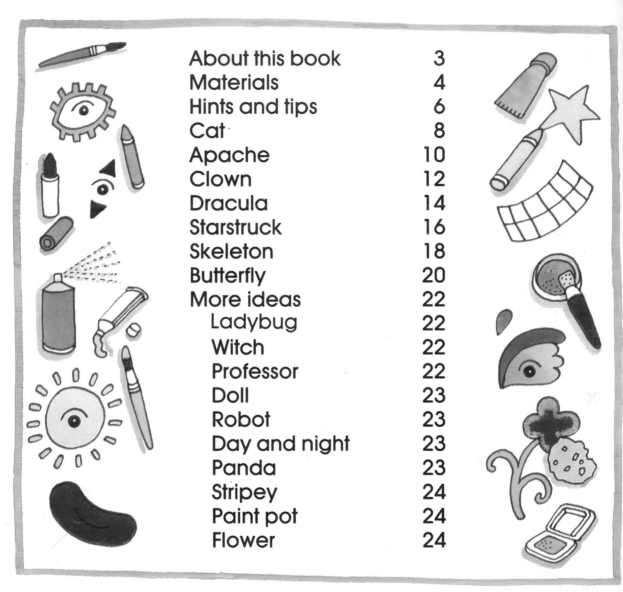

Produced by
Tony Potter, Times Four Publishing Ltd

Published by Warwick Press, 387 Park Avenue South,
New York, New York 10016, in 1990
Paperback edition published by Franklin Watts,
387 Park Avenue S., NY, NY

First published in 1990 by Grisewood & Dempsey Ltd,
London.

Typeset by TDR Photoset, Dartford
Colour separations by RCS Graphics Ltd
Printed in Spain

Conception and editorial:
Catherine Bruzzone, Multi Lingua

Library of Congress Cataloging-in-Publication Data

Beaton, Clare.
  Face painting / Clare Beaton.
    p. cm. – (Make and play)
    Summary: Describes the materials needed for face painting
provides step-by-step instructions for producing several des
Includes related activities.
    ISBN 0–531–15161–1   ISBN 0–531–19095–1 (lib. bdg
    1. Face painting – Juvenile literature. [1. Face painting.]
I. Title. II. Series.
TT911.B43 1990
745.5–dc20   90–1

About this book

This book will show you some easy and fun ways to paint your face. There are step-by-step instructions for seven main faces and ideas for lots more at the end of the book.

On the left-hand pages, there are four simple steps to follow:

On the right-hand pages, there is the finished face with some extra suggestions for you to try:

The simplest faces are at the beginning of the book and the more complicated ones at the end. Non-toxic face paints can be bought in most toy stores and some gift shops. Look at pages 4-7 for some other helpful suggestions.

You can do most of the faces very quickly, but you will need to plan, and perhaps shop, for some of the others. The extra faces at the end of the book do not have step-by-step instructions, but if you have tried the main faces you should find them easy to do.

Materials

You can buy various different kinds of face paints. The most common look like crayons but they can also be used with a brush (see page 6). You will find them in most toy stores.

☆ Theatrical makeup is more expensive but can give a better result and have more interesting colors. The larger theatrical suppliers have catalogs and sell by mail. Look them up in the telephone directory or ask at a local theater or drama club.

☆ It is fun to borrow old makeup and have a variety of lipsticks, eye shadows, glosses, pencils, and powders. Ask the owner first, of course! You could also buy cheap makeup from the drugstore.

☆ Make sure, especially with old makeup, that you are not allergic to it. Try a little first on the back of your hand or arm and leave it for a couple of hours. Don't use it if your skin goes blotchy or you get a rash.

☆ You can also find color sprays for your hair and skin. Ask in your drugstore. Follow the instructions for use very carefully. Be extra careful round your eyes with all paints, makeup, and sprays.

☆ Check that face paints are non-toxic. Try always to choose makeup which is non-allergen and has not been tested on animals. Look for "ozone-friendly" sprays.

☆ Your face will look best if you use a small sponge to put on a base color.

☆ Rub a moisturiser, like baby lotion, on your face before you start and the paint will wash off more easily. Use a flannel and water to clean your face. You may need soap to remove the darker colors — but be careful of your eyes!

Keep all face paints and makeup in a can or box and make sure the lids and caps are on firmly.

☆ Don't leave face paints in the sun or they will melt.

Hints and tips

The instructions in this book show a face painting crayon. Here are some other kinds of tools you can use to get different effects. You may find some of these already at home, but don't forget to ask the owner before using them.

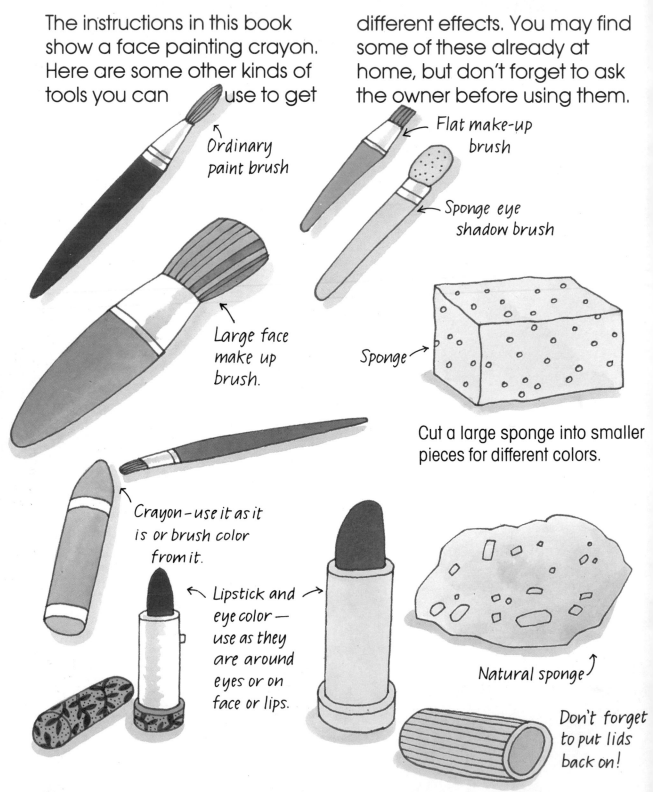

Ordinary paint brush

Flat make-up brush

Sponge eye shadow brush

Large face make up brush.

Sponge →

Cut a large sponge into smaller pieces for different colors.

Crayon – use it as it is or brush color from it.

← Lipstick and eye color — use as they are around eyes or on face or lips. →

Natural sponge

Don't forget to put lids back on!

Face painting can be very messy. Tie a towel or cloth around the neck and tie hair away from the face. A hair band or hair clips will do.

To paint a soft shape, use a sponge and very little color at the edges.

Draw the outline of the shape carefully with a brush and then fill in with color.

Fill in the outline with a contrasting color, or the same color as the outline.

Use a small brush to paint in extra details.

A large soft brush and powder can also soften the edges of color.

Cat

1 Use a sponge to color your face all over with white or orange face paint.

2 Draw a black nose.

3 Use black again to add whiskers.

4 Lastly, draw lots of stripes in black or brown.

Make some
ears out of
paper. Stick
them on to a hair
band or
piece of
elastic.

Tape
together.

Hair band

9

Apache

You can draw lots of different patterns to be an Apache. Here are two ideas:

1 Color your face light brown all over. Then draw some red lines.

2 Add some yellow lines next to the red ones.

1 First color your face light brown. Then draw a black wiggly line down one side.

2 Add red patterns on the other cheek and a white spot on your chin.

Stick a feather or two in the headband.

Make a head-band from a strip of patterned paper or material taped at the back.

If it's warm, you can also decorate your bare arms, hands and chest with more patterns.

11

Clown

Mind your eyes.

1 Use a sponge to color your face all over with white face paint.

2 Next, draw small triangles in black above and below each eye.

You could use a plastic nose instead.

3 Draw a round red nose.

4 Lastly, use black to draw a big smile around your mouth.

Make a tiny hat out of a yogurt tub. Clean and paint it or cover it in paper or foil. Thread thin elastic through it to hold it in place.

Wear a wig if you have one.

13

Dracula

Make your hair spiky with gel.

Mind your eyes. ⚡

1 Use a sponge to color your face all over with green face paint.

2 Draw large fierce eyebrows over your eyes with a dark color.

3 Next draw some long black scars on your cheeks and forehead.

4 Use red face paint to paint "blood" dripping from the corners of your mouth.

14

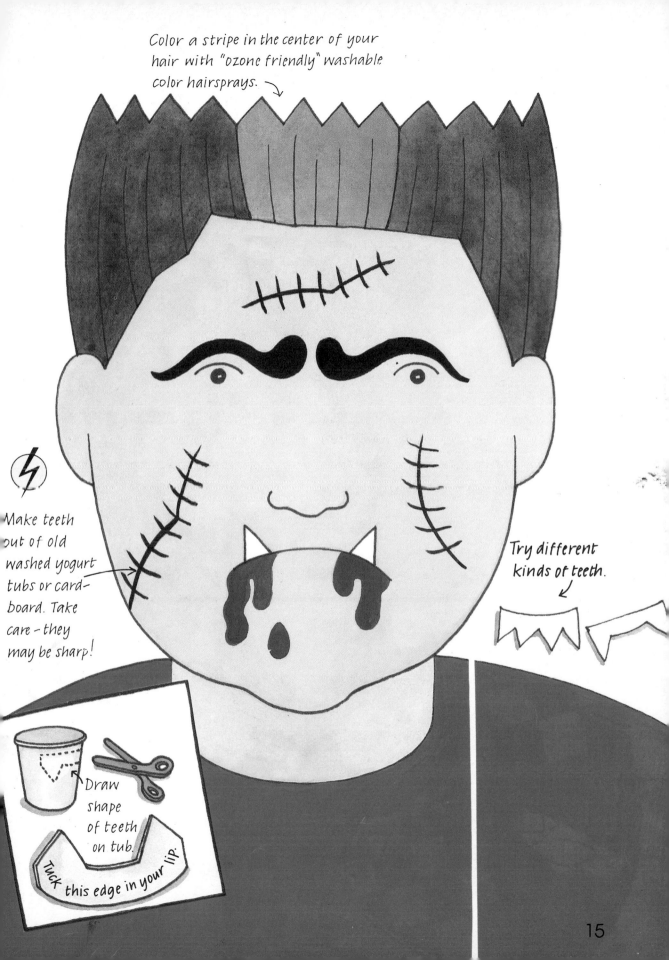

Color a stripe in the center of your hair with "ozone friendly" washable color hairsprays.

Make teeth out of old washed yogurt tubs or cardboard. Take care - they may be sharp!

Draw shape of teeth on tub.

Tuck this edge in your lip.

Try different kinds of teeth.

15

Starstruck

Be careful of your eyes when you color in the shapes.

1 Sponge your face all over with a pale color such as white, yellow or pink.

2 Draw black shapes around your eyes. Use a brush if possible.

3 Color in the shapes. Then draw a star outline on each cheek.

4 Lastly, finish coloring in and add spots.

Decorate your hair. Tie pieces up with hair bands, ribbons, and so on. →

Add stick-on jewels and glitter.

Color lips pink or blue.

Color your hair with "ozone friendly" washable color hairsprays. Make stripes in more than one color.

Skeleton

Make your hair spiky with hair gel. ↷

1 Use a sponge to color your face all over with white face paint.

⚡ Be careful of your eyes when you color around them.

2 Draw big, sad eye sockets. Add a small triangle on your nose.

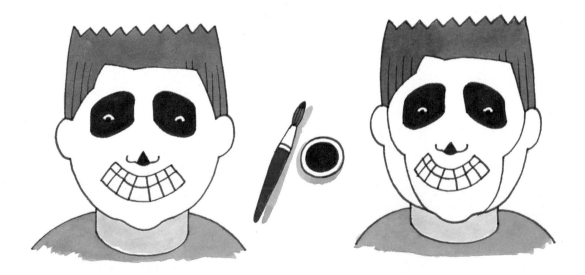

3 Next, use black to draw a wide smile. Draw in large teeth.

4 Lastly, draw the edge of the skeleton face in black.

Butterfly

1 Color your face all over with white face paint.

2 Draw the outline in a dark color such as blue.

3 Color in the wings and body using different colors.

4 Add purple spots to the lower wings.

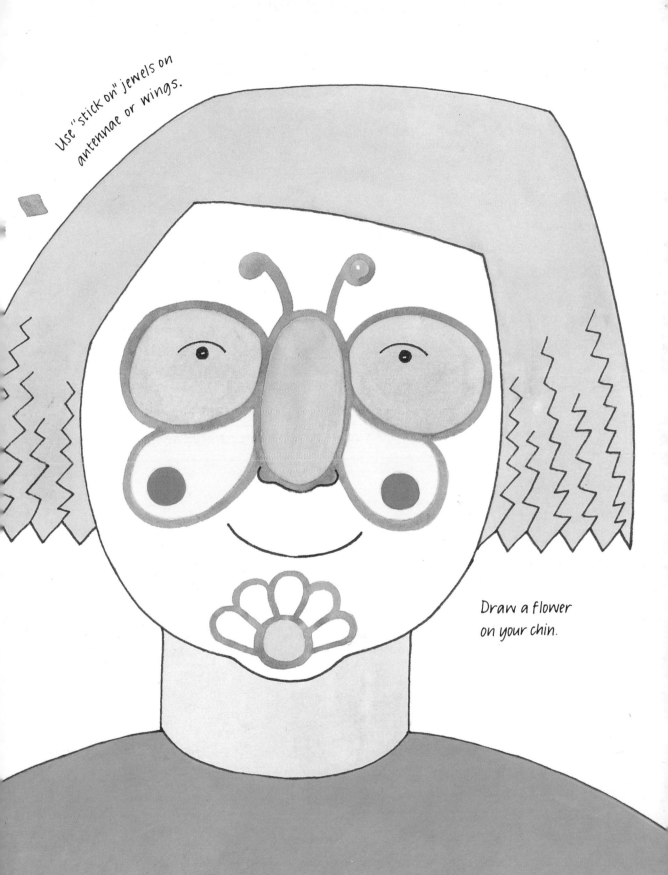

Use "stick on" jewels on antennae or wings.

Draw a flower on your chin.

More ideas

If you enjoyed the main ideas for painting your face, try a few more! There are no step-by-step instructions for the extra ideas on the next three pages, but the tips on pages 5 and 6 will help you with them.
There are also some extra costume ideas which will make your face painting look even better!

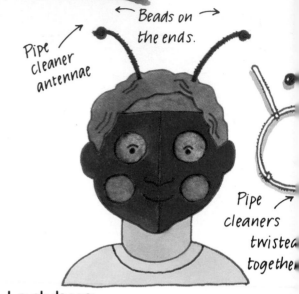

← Beads on the ends. →

Pipe cleaner antennae

Pipe cleaners twisted together

Ladybug
Paint a red face with black spots and black forehead.

Make a witch's hat from black paper.

You could wear plastic glasses instead

Wear a bow tie

Witch
Paint a green face with black eyebrows and purple stars.

Professor
Draw black glasses and a black mustache and beard.

Add a bow in your hair.

Black eyelashes.

Cover a pair of ear muffs with boxes and "springs" made from twisted pipe cleaners.

Make your hair spiky with hair gel.

Doll
Paint a white face and red cheeks and lips.

Robot
Paint a green face with square eyes and square lips.

Sun

Moon

Stars

Stick paper ears to a hair band.

Day and night
Halve your face in black and white. Decorate in yellow.

Panda
Paint a white face and black eyes and nose.

Paint the black lines very carefully with a brush.

Stripey
Start with a white face, then paint on black stripes. These pictures show different ideas you could try out.

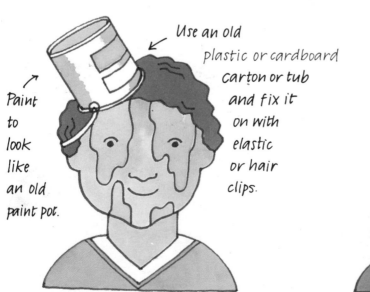

Paint to look like an old paint pot.

Use an old plastic or cardboard carton or tub and fix it on with elastic or hair clips.

Make the center a bright color

Paint pot
Paint your face one color then paint "drips" running down from a paint pot.

Flower
Paint a flower pattern, with your nose as the center. Draw petals around it.